RONA ARATO

illustrations by
CLAUDIA NEWELL

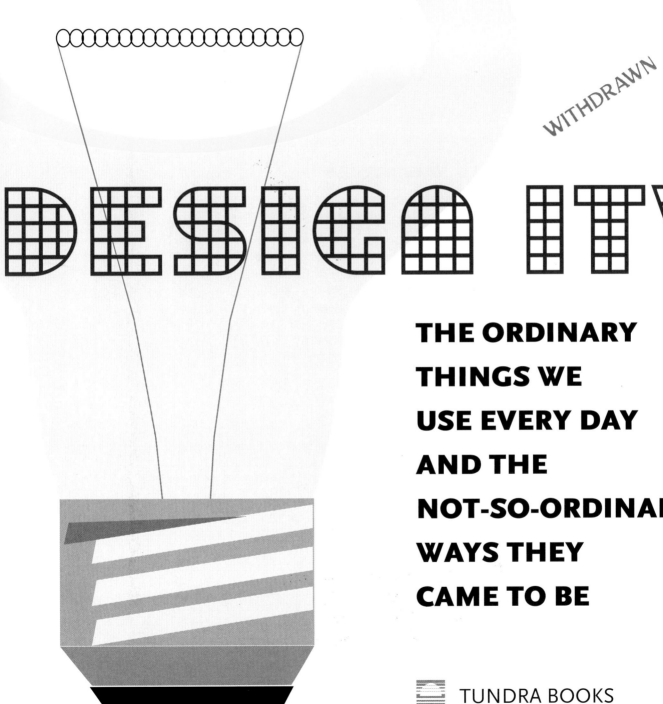

DESIGN IT!

THE ORDINARY THINGS WE USE EVERY DAY AND THE NOT-SO-ORDINARY WAYS THEY CAME TO BE

 TUNDRA BOOKS

To Paul, industrial designer extraordinaire – R.A.
To my parents, who shared their love of art and knowledge with me – C.N.

Published in Canada by Tundra Books,
75 Sherbourne Street, Toronto, Ontario M5A 2P9

Published in the United States by Tundra Books of Northern New York,
P.O. Box 1030, Plattsburgh, New York 12901

Library of Congress Control Number: 2009938453

Library and Archives Canada Cataloguing in Publication

Arato, Rona
    Design it: the ordinary things we use every day and the not-so-ordinary ways they came to be /
Rona Arato.

Includes bibliographical references.
ISBN 978-0-88776-846-0

    1. Design, Industrial—Juvenile literature. I. Title.

TS171.A73 2010   j745.2   C2008-902060-X

We acknowledge the financial support of the Government of Canada through the Book Publishing Industry Development Program (BPIDP) and that of the Government of Ontario through the Ontario Media Development Corporation's Ontario Book Initiative. We further acknowledge the support of the Canada Council for the Arts and the Ontario Arts Council for our publishing program.

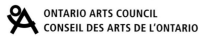

ONTARIO ARTS COUNCIL
CONSEIL DES ARTS DE L'ONTARIO

Design by Andrew Roberts

Printed in China

1 2 3 4 5 6   15 14 13 12 11 10

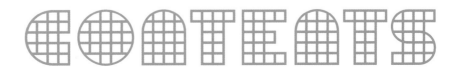

CHAPTER ONE

PROBLEM SOLVER + DREAMER = INDUSTRIAL DESIGNER

HAVE YOU EVER THOUGHT *boy, this bike seat is uncomfortable* or *my cup of hot chocolate's too hot to hold* or *it takes so long for me to brush my teeth.* If you thought *maybe an adjustable bike seat would make my bike more comfortable,* or *a sleeve around my hot chocolate would let me hold it without burning my hands,* or *maybe a battery in my toothbrush would help me clean my teeth,* you are thinking like an **industrial designer**. From the home you live in to the furniture you use, the computer that keeps you connected and the toys you like best, your life has been affected by industrial design.

4

THE WAY IT WAS....

A revolution happens when people replace one sysyem with another. In this case, the Industrial Revolution in the 1700s introduced factories that had machines that made things faster and cheaper than people could by hand. This major change is called mass production. For instance, cloth woven in factories became highly prized.

Is the wheel turning again? Do we prize handmade things more nowadays? The profession of industrial design developed from the need to find a balance between art and industry.

THE WAY IT IS NOW....

WHAT'S GOOD INDUSTRIAL DESIGN?

Good design adds a *WOW!* factor to a product. It combines the right choice of materials, colors, details, and proportions that make you want to buy and use the product. Well-designed products are easy to operate and do what they are meant to do.

A *Good Design* **Checklist**

 ## FUNCTION
GOOD DESIGN ENSURES THE PRODUCT SHOWS YOU WHAT IT DOES

Industrial designers say that the *form* should show you its *function* – it should look like what it does. The two wheels, handlebars, and pedals show you that a bicycle is made to ride. A small bike that has three wheels is a tricycle, and its form tells you that it is meant for young children.

 ## USABILITY
GOOD DESIGN KEEPS THE USER IN MIND

Does the design work for the person who uses the product? Think about the things you've used that aren't right for you anymore: your crib, your diapers, and your rattle. A good designer studies the age, size, strength, and interests of the people who would use a product to make sure there's a good fit.

DESIGNING FOR "REAL" PEOPLE

Henry Dreyfuss, a pioneer of industrial design, spent a lot of time studying the human figure because he believed that machines should be adapted to the way people are built. His ideas became the technical discipline called human factors. Human factors began during the Second World War to develop standards for the design of military equipment. Today, designers use these principles to make products safe, comfortable, and the best they can be for the people who will use them.

HENRY FORD (JULY 30, 1863 – APRIL 7, 1947)

Henry Ford established the Ford Motor Company, a car manufacturing company, in 1903. But at that time, only rich people could afford cars because just a few could be made in a day, by small groups of two or three people. In 1908, Ford introduced the Model T, which was made on the first conveyor-belt assembly line, with workers adding one part to each of the cars that went down the line. Because the Ford Motor Company could produce more Ford Model Ts daily, the cost went down and more people could afford to buy a Ford.

☑ ERGONOMICS
GOOD DESIGN WORKS WELL

Industrial designers must understand ergonomics, the science of making things workable. The word comes from the Greek word *ergon*, which means, "to work." Designers use ergonomic principles to make products safe, comfortable, and easy to use. Ergonomic principles determine the shape of a chair, the controls on a video game console, and even the seats in a car!

☑ AESTHETICS
GOOD DESIGN LOOKS GREAT

Aesthetics refer to how appealing something looks. Designers choose shapes, colors, and textures that make a product as attractive as possible. But what makes a product eye-catching can vary depending on the time, place, and tastes of the people who use it. People used to love their avocado-colored kitchen appliances. Now we go for stainless steel. Industrial designers watch for trends in taste.

☑ GOOD DESIGN IS GREEN DESIGN

Green design is kind to the environment. It uses materials that are safe and biodegradable. It uses minimal energy. A green product can be used by more than one person.

CAST OF CHARACTERS

Industrial designers work with a team of professionals. These include engineers, molders, suppliers, and model makers.

WHAT IS AN INDUSTRIAL DESIGNER?

An industrial designer is a trained professional who creates and develops concepts for new products. The designer's job is to make a product look and work the best it can, so that both the manufacturer *and* the user benefit from it. Industrial designers need a degree in Industrial Design. As students, they study drafting, sketching, computer-aided design (CAD), manufacturing methods, and tools and industrial materials. Designers are good in mathematics, and many have a background in engineering.

WHAT DOES AN ENGINEER DO?

Engineers use mathematical and scientific principles to ensure that products are strong and safe and made from the proper materials.

WHAT IS A MOLDER?

Molds are the forms used to shape a product. Think of a muffin tin. A molder is the person who makes the mold used to form the round shape of the muffin tin and other products.

WHAT IS A SUPPLIER?

A supplier is the person who sells the materials used to make products.

WHAT IS A MODEL MAKER?

Model makers are sculptors and artists who bring a product concept to life. They know a lot about materials, tools, and manufacturing techniques, and they help designers figure out what will work best for their products. Model makers must have a sense of scale (the ability to picture a full-sized object smaller) and be able to think about things in three dimensions. They must have a passion for detail and know what materials to use for specific models. A good model is a work of art!

TRICKS OF THE TRADE

HOW DOES AN INDUSTRIAL DESIGNER WORK?

The industrial designer is the link between the customer and the manufacturer who makes and sells the product. Industrial designers are artists, inventors, and dreamers, who come up with ideas for new and existing products. They use pencils, paper, markers, and computer-aided design programs (CAD) to create sketches and renderings (three-dimensional drawings) of the products. The designer works with the company's engineers and marketing staff to create safe, attractive products that people want to buy and use.

HOW DO DESIGNERS TEST THEIR PRODUCTS?

Designers are always learning. They create many versions of a product, based on its function. With each new version, the product evolves and gets better. Once a product is made, designers test it to see how it works. The people in the company's marketing department will use the product to see what they like or dislike about it. They ask focus groups of consumers what they like and don't like. They invite kids to be toy testers. This process is called test marketing. The designer will improve the design based on the user feedback. Almost every product you use has been tested. Do people want toothpaste that tastes minty or like garlic? Do folks prefer bubble gum that's pink or sludge brown?

HOW DO DESIGNERS PROTECT THEIR PRODUCTS?

Designers and inventors spend a great deal of time and money developing new products, and they want to protect them, so that other people or companies can't use their designs without permission. To do that, a designer applies for a patent. The product must have new features or special functions that haven't been patented before. The patent grants the designer a property right, or ownership, which prevents other people from making and selling the same product for twenty years.

A patent protects the way a product works. A design patent protects the way it looks. A trademark is a word, name, or symbol, such as "Rollerblade," that distinguishes a certain product so that its name comes to represent an entire category of products. Rollerblades were the first brand of in-line skates, and people started to call any form of in-line skating rollerblading. Can you think of other examples where this has happened?

9

CHAPTER TWO

KEEP IT COZY: DESIGN FOR HOMES

HOW COMFORTABLE, COZY, AND WELCOMING your home is owes a lot to an army of industrial designers.

THE WAY IT WAS....

Our earliest ancestors lived in caves. Nature's design was pretty good. Caves sheltered people from the elements: rain, snow, wind, and excessive heat, and they protected them from wild animals that roamed the earth. Caves were practical because they didn't have to be designed or built, and they had ideal temperatures for storing foods such as fruits and nuts.

But one thing made them impractical. A cave pretty much stays put. If a group had to follow herds of animals to new grazing grounds or to look for fresh water, they needed to take their homes with them wherever they went. To do this, ancient people learned how to make tents of stretched animal hides or fabrics on wooden poles. They could fold up their tents and transport them to a new location where there was more game or fresh water.

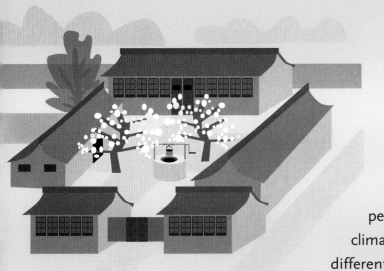

Once the earliest civilizations began to grow their own crops, using seeds from plants that they found in the wild, people no longer needed to keep moving, and they built permanent housing. Because of various climates around the world, people had to build different types of houses to suit their environments, with the tools that were available to them.

In northern Europe and northern China, people built *hearth houses* or huts with one room that was square or round. A fire was made on a stone hearth in the middle of the room, and the smoke blew out through the roof. Because of the cold and wet weather, rooftops had to be sloped so that rain or snow could run down to the ground. And for extra warmth, animals were often kept inside.

In Egypt, south Asia, and southern China, the climate was hot most of the time, so people had to build homes that stayed cool. Wood was scarce, so they built *courtyard homes* made from mud-brick. Mud-brick houses had walls with small rooms built in and an open courtyard in the center that had a well in its middle.

By 3000 BC, people in West Asia, Greece, and Rome had become wealthier, so they were able to build better houses. That gave rise to a new profession called "architecture." Architects design buildings. In Greece, people included the basics that are in most homes today: more rooms, brick floors, cupboards, and tiled rooftops. These houses often had grand pillars in front.

By the 13th century, European villages were centers of trade, and houses kept citizens and their livestock safe from nomads who plundered the countryside. Soon, many people began to abandon farming and move to towns and villages to become merchants. Towns grew into cities, and then those cities became crowded. By the 1800s, apartments were constructed as a solution to the overcrowding.

A Home Design *Checklist*

☑ **FORM AND FUNCTION**

DOES IT LOOK LIKE A HOME?

Whether it's a cabin or a mansion, a home has to be a safe, comfortable, relaxing place to live. It would look much different from a prison or an office or a classroom.

☑ **USABILITY**

DOES IT DO WHAT IT'S SUPPOSED TO DO?

It keeps you safe and comfortable. It has areas to cook in, sleep in, go to the bathroom in, wash in – all the activities we associate with home. It's got enough space for all the people in it. And it's affordable for the folks who are housed there.

☑ **ERGONOMICS**

DO ALL THE PARTS, FROM ROOF TO CELLAR, WORK?

The heating, the lighting, and the plumbing are all efficient. The rooms are laid out in a sensible way. You wouldn't choose to have your kitchen too far from where you eat or your bedrooms near a recreation room, where it's likely to be noisy.

AESTHETICS

DOES IT LOOK GREAT?

Tastes change, but everybody, no matter the size or cost of their home, wants it to look as nice as it can. Do you like old houses or sleek new lofts? A cabin in the woods, or a floating houseboat? All of them can be good homes.

IS IT GREEN?

Designers and architects look for ways to make homes energy efficient. Solar panels on roofs convert sunlight to energy. Modern doors and windows are designed to seal in heat and keep out cold air. Is your house as energy efficient as it can be? What can you do to make it even more energy efficient?

THE "CHIMNEY EFFECT"

When you see smoke curling out of a chimney, it's because of a principle called "the chimney effect." When you light a fire in a fireplace, the heat warms the air above it. Since warm air is light, it rises. Chimneys are built above fireplaces so that the hot air is funnelled up through them and drawn outside of the house.

THE WAY IT IS NOW....

WHO DESIGNED YOUR HOUSE?

Whether you live in an apartment, a house, or a motor home, an architect designed your home. An architect is someone who designs structures (homes, malls, museums, and even stadiums) and determines how the space is used within them. Architects work with engineers to make sure the building is safe *and* functional, meaning that the space should be made for its purpose. This is a huge responsibility. The design of a school building is different from the design of a house, and those designs differ from one for a mall.

THUMBS UP! *USONIAN HOMES*
FRANK LLOYD WRIGHT (JUNE 8, 1867-APRIL 9, 1959)

Born in Wisconsin, Frank Lloyd Wright was an American architect, designer, writer, and educator who developed a completely new style of architecture. In 1887, he moved to Chicago, where he joined an architectural firm. After several years, he started his own firm in his home in Oak Park, Illinois.

Wright thought that the form of a building should be practical and express its function. As an early advocate of solar heating, he believed that architects should appreciate the beauty of nature and use it in their designs. In 1901, Wright began designing homes in what he called *Prairie Style*. His design for these houses mirrored the flat, spacious Prairie land, with an open plan that included wide doorways, open rooms, neat exteriors, and sloping roofs. This style remains an inspiration to architects of the past and present.

In the 1930s, Wright designed less expensive houses for middle-class families. These *Usonian* houses were practical, user-friendly, and they made use of local materials such as stone and wood. Cars were able to park beneath an overhang jutting out from the roof – a design that is known as a *carport*.

WHAT'S THE GLITCH? *COST!*

HABITAT 67

Habitat 67 in Montreal, Quebec, was a great and innovative design for its time, but in the end, it proved to be too expensive for designers to use on other buildings.

Designed as an exhibit for Montreal's Expo 67, architect Moshe Safdie wanted to build a garden-style, multi-family complex that made maximum use of the land, while providing the openness of suburban homes. The complex is twelve storeys of terraced apartments, with over a hundred apartments arranged in setback steps. The units were formed first and then taken to a second location, where the rooms, such as kitchens and bathrooms, were installed. When the units were completed, each one was moved to the Habitat site and lifted into place by a crane. The completed units weighed between 70-90 tons! What makes Habitat unique is the way the apartments are grouped to look like a town built on the side of a hill. Each unit is placed on the roof of the apartment below it. There are elevators in a central core, and playgrounds are on the top floor.

After the exposition closed, Habitat became a regular apartment building. Although it was considered a success, it cost a great deal more to build than conventional tower-style apartment buildings. It has never been duplicated; however, many architects have studied it and continue to learn from Safdie's intricate design.

THINK LIKE AN INDUSTRIAL DESIGNER

When building structures, architects always start by drawing a *floor plan*. Look around your own home. What rooms does it have? Most homes have a living room, dining room, bedrooms, a kitchen, and a bathroom. On a piece of paper, draw a floor plan for your ideal house.

Your house can be as big or as small as you'd like. Is your home one-storey or two? Think about how many rooms you'd like to put in your home, and how each room would be used. How many bedrooms do you need? How many bathrooms? How big is your living room? Is there a fireplace? Is your television in the living room or in a family room? Do you need a separate office space or will a smaller study area suit your needs? If you like to cook, you may want a big kitchen with lots of counter space where you can prepare food and keep small appliances.

How green is your home? Do you have lots of windows for natural lighting? Do you have solar panels to generate electricity? Is there a garden in front or in the back? How about a pool? Do you have one entrance or a front and back entrance? How about a driveway and a garage?

Now that you've designed your home, think about the furniture you'll need. What kind of window coverings will you have? Will you have hardwood floors or carpets? Now look at your plan. Have you designed it to be the very best it can be?

CHAPTER THREE

SPLISH, SPLASH, LET'S TAKE A BATH: DESIGN FOR BATHROOMS

INDUSTRIAL DESIGNERS HAVE TRANSFORMED THE WAY WE KEEP CLEAN.

THE WAY IT WAS....

Ancient Romans loved to bathe, but most citizens had to bathe in public bathhouses, in pools of dirty water. In those times, royalty and the wealthy bathed more than the average person did, and their facilities were private; they stood in a basin while servants poured cold water over them. By the 1400s, most cities in Europe still used public bathhouses where people paid to bathe. In fact, many bathhouses in Paris had town criers who stood outside and called out when the bathwater was hot. Those who lived in the countryside had to get their water from a river or well and heat it over a fire or on the stove. They could only bathe in a large wooden bucket once a week or less, and, often, a whole family took turns using the same bathwater.

Modern showers first came into use late in the 18th century. People had to pull a cord that spurted cold water from an overhead tank, pouring it directly onto the bather. The blast of the cold water was so jarring that most people continued to warm their water to use in tubs. In 1898, Edwin Ruud invented the first hot-water tank, and his technology has progressed so that today we have indoor plumbing and plenty of hot water.

THANK YOU MR. CUMMINGS, INVENTOR OF THE TOILET!

Before there were indoor toilets, people used to go to the bathroom in chamber pots, which were kept under the bed and emptied every morning. Sometimes, people threw the contents out an open window. *Yech!*

In some places, people had outhouses, which are still used today at campsites and other outdoor facilities.

Watchmaker Alexander Cummings invented the first flush toilet in 1775. His toilet had a separate water tank high above the seat, and to flush it, you pulled on a chain. Joseph Bramah later improved on this design, and Thomas Crapper manufactured Bramah's new-and-improved toilet.

THE WAY IT IS NOW....

Designers and engineers have advanced the toilet design by bringing the water tank down, making it part of the toilet. This makes it more efficient and easier to install and maintain. When designing a toilet, the designer takes into account how high the seat should be, what shape it should be, and how to make it comfortable.

A *Bathroom Design* Checklist

☑ FORM AND FUNCTION

DOES IT REFLECT WHAT YOU USE IT FOR?

There's running water, waterproof surfaces, and privacy around you, all the things you want in a bathroom. Modern bathtubs are mostly made of waterproof materials such as steel that is layered with enamel to prevent rust, and some are made of acrylic or fiberglass plastics.

☑ USABILITY

DOES IT ALLOW US TO DO WHAT WE NEED TO DO IN A BATHROOM?

In North America, we like to take care of all our bathroom needs in one place, so our bathrooms typically have a sink, a toilet, and bathtub or shower. Not so in other parts of the world, where the toilet and a small sink get a room of their own.

Industrial designers keep safety in mind. Does the toilet have to be high to accommodate people with mobility needs or low for younger folk? We all need non-slip surfaces.

Is it easy to keep clean?

☑ ERGONOMICS

DO ALL THE PARTS WORK TO MAKE IT SAFE, WARM OR COLD, AND WATERPROOF?

It makes lots of hot water available. The surfaces and features don't allow leaks into other parts of the house. It is ventilated to keep it free of mildew and odor.

☑ AESTHETICS

DOES IT LOOK GREAT?

We like to relax in our bathrooms, so the surfaces and colors should be pleasing to our eyes.

☑ IS IT GREEN?

A green bathroom is a clean and efficient bathroom. Here are some tips for greening your bathroom and helping the environment:

- Install a low-flow showerhead to save water.
- Buy towels made from organic cotton.
- Use toilet paper made from recycled paper.
- Turn off the water while you brush your teeth.
- Unclog drains.
- Fix leaky faucets.
- Use a (PVC) polyvinyl-chloride-free shower curtain.

RAYMOND LOEWY (NOVEMBER 5, 1893 - JULY 14, 1986)

Raymond Loewy is considered the father of modern industrial design. He developed the design style *streamlining* to make products with smooth surfaces. Loewy contoured the bodies of products such as bathroom fixtures, dishes, and furniture to make them sleek, comfortable, and easy to clean and use. From the 1930s to the 1970s, he streamlined many products. He even streamlined gigantic objects such as ocean liners, airplanes, and trains. One of his most famous designs is the original Coca-Cola bottle. It was made of green glass and designed to resemble the shape of a woman's body.

21

THUMBS UP!

Shower stalls are better for people with disabilities and for seniors because they are made with doors that make it easy to get in and out. Some also have metal handrails to help people stand without slipping.

WHAT'S THE GLITCH? *SAFETY AND COMFORT*

Bathtubs with a poor design have high sides, which make it difficult for someone to step into. There are often no handrails to hang on to. Tubs can also be uncomfortable if the backs are not slanted.

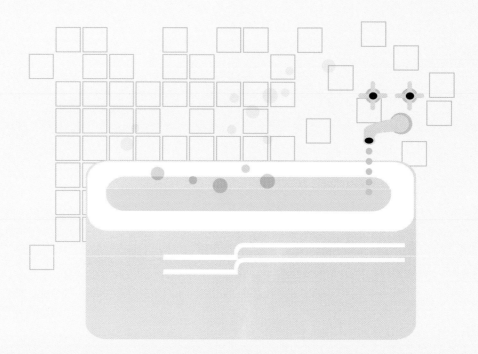

THINK LIKE AN INDUSTRIAL DESIGNER

MAKE YOUR BATHROOM USER-FRIENDLY

Does your bathtub have a slip-proof surface? If not, use a rubber bath mat or adhesive decals so you won't slip in the tub. Your floor rugs should have rubber backing so that they don't slide. If you don't already have them, ask your parents to install grab handles on the bathtub wall to make it easier and safer to get in and out of it. If you have glass shower doors, ask your parents if the glass is shatterproof.

CHAPTER FOUR

FROM CAMPFIRES TO MICROWAVE OVENS AND OTHER COOL / HOT STUFF: DESIGN FOR KITCHENS

THE WAY IT WAS....
STOVES – HOT STUFF!

Tens of thousands of years ago, people learned how to start and use fire. It kept people warm, gave them light, and allowed them to cook their food. No one knows exactly how or when, but the discovery was probably an accident such as a lightning strike. Fire was the single most important discovery in history – our ability to manipulate and use it allowed us to further civilization. No wonder so many early civilizations believed that fire was a gift from the gods and used it in their ceremonies and celebrations.

By 6000 BC, people learned how to bring fire indoors. At first they built their fires on dirt floors that lay in the middle of their homes. Back then, a house would have a hole in the roof for smoke and sparks to drift out. But the smoke was overpowering, and everything inside the house was always covered in soot. To solve this, people built fireplaces with chimneys to hold the open fire in and to send the smoke outside.

When people cooked over an open fire or in a fireplace, they had to be careful not to burn themselves or catch their clothing on fire. Stoves were invented to contain fire, to make cooking faster, and to heat a room safely and efficiently.

Stoves have had many different designs and were made with several materials – from earthenware tiles to ceramics to cast iron. But it was the invention of the metal stove in the 1800s that paved the way for today's modern ranges. Benjamin Franklin invented the Franklin stove in 1742, but he had designed it for heating a room, not for cooking. In the 19th century, Benjamin Thompson improved Franklin's design, creating the first kitchen stove with a built-in oven. Back then, stoves used wood or coal. Today's stoves are powered by either gas or electricity.

THE WAY IT IS NOW....

Cooking is so much easier and safer than it used to be. Modern appliances and cooking utensils have improved a lot since our ancestors cooked over open fires. Stoves are now made of fireproof materials such as steel. They have smooth surfaces that are easy to clean. Most stoves are approximately 3.5 feet (1 meter) tall, so the cook can comfortably reach the pots and pans. Some stoves have the dials at the back, which keeps them out of the reach of children. But to use these dials the cook has to reach over the hot burners. Other stoves have dials in front, making them easier to use, but it also means that they are accessible to children. As a solution, stoves can be built onto the flat surface of a countertop. That way, the stove is at waist height for the average person, and the dials are beside their respective burners. Now you don't have to reach over a hot element, and the dials are safely out of reach of small children.

REFRIGERATION – A REALLY COOL STORY

In the early 1800s, Englishman Michael Faraday learned how to cool things with liquid ammonia gas. Modern refrigerators use a compression refrigeration system based on Mr. Faraday's experiments. Compressed gas is sent through coils that cool and expand it. The coils used to be on the top of refrigerators, but today they are hidden at the back.

Once most people had stoves and refrigerators, they wanted other time-saving appliances. Toasters, blenders, and microwave ovens are just a few of the appliances that have been developed over the years to make cooking easier, safer, and more fun.

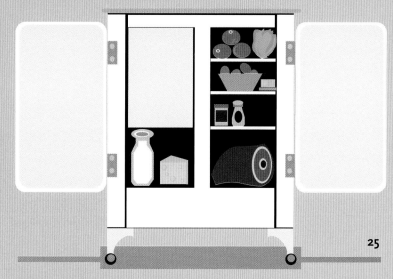

ACCESSORIZE YOUR KITCHEN
MICROWAVE OVENS

Did you know that microwave ovens were invented by accident? In 1946, Dr. Percy Spencer worked for the Raytheon Company, which designed a vacuum tube, called a magnetron, that generated electromagnetic radiation called microwaves. He realized that when he had chocolate in his pocket and walked past the magnetron, the microwaves melted the chocolate. He wondered if they would also cook food. He experimented and found that not only did the microwaves cook food, but they were able to do it fast. Dr. Spencer's discovery led to the invention of microwave ovens.

At first, commercial microwave ovens were too expensive for people to buy and too big to fit into a home kitchen. They were approximately 5.5 feet tall (1.7 meters), weighed over 750 pounds (340 kilograms), and cost around $5,000. Raytheon kept designing smaller and more efficient models, and in 1967, they introduced the first countertop microwave oven for around $500. Microwave ovens meant faster, safer meal preparation. Today they outsell traditional stoves because they can be used in more places.

TRICKS OF THE TRADE

Improvements can come by accident like the microwave or by taking an idea like a lightbulb and applying it to something entirely different – like toasting bread.

TOASTERS

Before toasters were invented, to toast bread you had to spear it with a fork and hold it over an open fire or the stove top. There were various toaster designs before the invention of electricity in the 1800s. But once electricity was available, inventors were determined to find ways to bring it into the home.

Electric toasters came along in the early 1900s when an engineer named Albert Marsh discovered that a mixture of nickel and chromium produced the type of wire needed to heat a slice of bread. In 1926, engineer Charles Strite added springs and a timer to the invention to create the Toastmaster, the first automatic pop-up toaster. In 1930, the Continental Baking Company introduced pre-sliced bread, making the Toastmaster a household standard.

BLENDERS

Whether your favorite milkshake is chocolate, vanilla, or strawberry, it was made in a blender. Blenders were the first kitchen appliances to use motors. Stephen Poplawski invented the first crude blender in 1922. Fred Waring refined his design and introduced the Waring Blender in 1937. His blender had a large glass container, a stainless-steel base, and a motor that turned a blade in the bottom of the container. By 1954, one million Waring Blenders were sold. The design was so successful that the original blender is still sold today.

Blenders are designed with features like removable blades. Some have push buttons while others have switches or touch pads. Their jars can be made from glass, polycarbonate, or stainless steel.

CUTLERY

Well into the Middle Ages people used slabs of bread as plates, knives, and wooden spoons. The fork became commonplace in the 11th century in Greece, Italy, and France. But before forks were adopted by the masses, they were found only in the homes of nobility. At first, they were made with only two tines, but later, they would be made with up to five tines. Back then, forks were mainly used to hold meat steady while it was carved. By the 1600s, forks were widely used throughout Europe by both the rich and poor. Soon, more ornately carved utensils were made, and they came in sets that included a serving fork. Cutlery became valuable and was often placed in wills and passed on from generation to generation.

A *Kitchen Design Checklist*

FORM AND FUNCTION
DOES IT REFLECT WHAT YOU USE IT FOR?

It's all about food. A kitchen should have places to store, prepare, and cook food – and sometimes to eat it too.

USABILITY
DOES IT LET YOU DO ALL THE THINGS YOU NEED TO DO IN THE SPACE?

Can you fry, bake, roast, or broil? Warm things up, keep them cool, and even freeze them? Do the sharp, dangerous machines we use have a place to operate and to be stored safely? Is your kitchen just for you and a parent? A galley kitchen might be plenty for your needs. Not so if you're part of a big family of kids, parents, and grandparents!

ERGONOMICS
DO ALL THE PARTS WORK TO MAKE IT SAFE AND EFFICIENT?

Have you ever used a fork that bent when you stabbed a piece of meat? Can you turn on the stove without burning yourself? Are sharp tools such as knives stored in safe places? Are electrical outlets a safe distance from the sink? Can you wash your dishes without flooding the folks in the apartment below? Is your food kept safe from creepy crawlies? Is the counter at a comfortable height?

AESTHETICS

DOES IT LOOK GREAT?

Is your kitchen a cheerful, pleasant place to work? Is it free of clutter? Bright colors make it feel light and airy. Look at pictures of old kitchens to see how taste in color has changed. In the 1950s, pink refrigerators were popular. What color is your refrigerator? Does it match your stove?

IS IT GREEN?

Think "green" to make your kitchen environmentally friendly. Recycle, reduce, reuse. Are your stove, refrigerator, and other appliances energy-saving models? Do you unplug small appliances such as toasters when they're not in use? Do you use your conventional oven just to bake a potato? Instead, use a toaster oven or microwave oven. Save energy whenever you can.

OXO

OXO was founded by Sam Farber in 1990 on the philosophy of universal design — creating products that are easy to use for the largest group of users. Farber's wife had arthritis in her hands and had trouble using many kitchen utensils. Farber wanted to create ergonomically designed kitchen tools that were easy for everyone to use. With the firm Smart Design, Farber conducted research that included talking to consumers, chefs, and retailers who sold kitchen utensils. He also worked with a gerontologist (a professional who works with the elderly) to understand the requirements of people with special needs. Then they designed and tested many models of each product to make sure they were safe and ergonomic.

OXO introduced a line of fifteen kitchen utensils, including peelers, potato mashers, and measuring utensils. Today, OXO manufactures hundreds of ergonomic products.

THUMBS UP!

Who knew there were so many ways to peel a carrot? Designers wanted to make a peeler that would be easy for everyone to use, whether they are right- or left-handed. They studied how people in different countries use peelers and found that in Japan and Europe, most people peel toward themselves, using their thumb for stability. In North America, most people peel away from themselves. Through their studies, the designers were able to create a tool that is comfortable for everyone to use, whichever way they choose to peel.

WHAT'S THE GLITCH? *ERGONOMICS*

Vegetable peelers can be hard to hold. Some designs have handles with sharp edges that cut into the user's hand, or blades that wobble back and forth so they don't grip the peel.

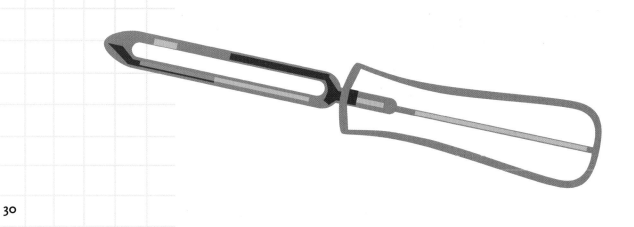

THINK LIKE AN INDUSTRIAL DESIGNER

Ask your parents to let you do an inventory of your kitchen drawers. Are the utensils ergonomic? Are any of them hard to hold? Are they rusty? Can you design a tool to keep kitchen drawers organized?

LEFT-HANDED TOOLS

Ten percent of all people today are left-handed, but scientists don't think that has always been the case. Implements found by archaeologists are divided equally between right- and left-handedness. But at some point, a preference for the right hand emerged.

Some religions associated being left-handed with evil, and "lefties" were accused of being witches or devil-worshippers. Left-handed people were forced to use their right hands, and they were punished if they did not. Historically, many inventions were engineered for right-handed people: tools, appliances, and furniture are just some of them. As a result, left-handed people have trouble using everyday instruments.

Today, doctors and scientists know more about hand preference, which is thought to be hereditary. Lefties can now find specially designed tools.

They now face less stigma and fewer obstacles. However, in some parts of the world being left-handed is still considered a handicap. As attitudes continue to change, and doctors and scientists learn more about the gene pool, more and more tools are designed for the left hand or for use in either hand.

31

CHAPTER FIVE

PULL UP A CHAIR: DESIGN FOR FURNITURE

THE WAY IT WAS...

Remember those early houses where people cooked over fires in the middle of the floor? Well, in those days, there was no furniture. People slept on the ground. For mattresses, they used piles of leaves, straw, sticks, and animal skins that were often filled with bugs. *Ugh*.

Around 3600 BC, pharaohs in Egypt figured out that by raising a flat piece of wood off the ground, they could protect themselves from crawly things that scrambled over them at night. The common people, however, could not afford such an extravagance, and they continued to sleep on piles of insect-infested straw in the corners of their homes.

The Romans found a way to stuff a cloth cover (called a ticking) with hay, reeds, and feathers to make a mattress – the first luxury bed. When people learned how to make and use tools, they began making simple furniture such as tables, three-legged stools, and beds. People became more skilled and began to make fancier furniture. Before the industrial revolution, furniture was hand-made by artisans or craftspeople. Today, most of our furniture comes from factories, and industrial designers create it.

Believe it or not, before the 16th century, chairs were a symbol of authority and reserved for royalty and the very powerful. Common folk rarely owned or sat in them. Ancient Egyptian and Greek rulers had chairs made of materials such as ebony, ivory, marble, and gilded wood. They were elaborately decorated with gems and other coverings, and the legs were usually carved in the shape of powerful animals to symbolize the strength and divinity of the ruler.

THE WAY IT IS NOW....

Today we use furniture for all parts of our lives. We sleep in beds and sit on chairs. We eat at tables and work at desks.

Cribs became popular in the 1800s. Early infant beds were cradles. They usually had curved rockers on the bottom so that parents could rock their babies. Most cradles were crafted by woodworkers. Today's cribs are still designed by woodworkers, but they are made in factories. There are strict ergonomic safety rules for their design to ensure that babies are not injured.

- **The bars are close together so babies can't stick their heads through them.**

- **The solid headboard and footboard keep their heads, toes, and fingers inside the crib.**

- **A snug-fitting mattress keeps babies safe.**

- **Small parts such as nails and screws are secure and well hidden.**

- **There are no loose pieces for babies to swallow.**

CHAIR DESIGN

Chairs are a necessity in our daily lives. We sit on them to eat, read, rest, relax, and work. They take the weight off our legs and support our backs and bums. The first thing a chair designer must consider is how someone will use it. Will he or she use it to sit in front of a computer or in front of a television? Is it a high chair for a baby? Is it a chair you'll lounge on in your backyard? Its purpose determines how it will be made.

IKEA

IKEA founder Ingvar Kamprad was born, in 1926, in Sweden, and raised on a farm called Elmtaryd, near the village of Agunnaryd. He started his business at the age of seventeen and used his initials plus those of his farm and village to form the name IKEA. He sold all kinds of goods but soon settled on furniture produced by local manufacturers. He began advertising and published a catalogue. Two years later, he opened a showroom so people could see and test out the furniture before buying it. Kamprad opened a store with display space, and it was the largest store in Scandinavia. He began designing his own furniture, which he sold at lower prices than his competitors did. An IKEA employee, Gillis Lundgren, had removed the legs from a table so it would fit into a car, and he approached Kamprad with his idea: IKEA furniture would be knocked-down (in pieces), so it could fit into flat boxes. With flat boxes, IKEA was able to ship more furniture in one truck, use less storage space, and reduce damage. People saved money because they could take home their own furniture instead of having it delivered.

Today there are IKEA stores all over the world, and many companies design ready-to-assemble furniture.

A *Furniture Design* *Checklist*

 ## FORM AND FUNCTION
DOES IT REFLECT WHAT YOU USE IT FOR?
A bed should be flat so you can lie down on it. A chair needs four legs, a seat, and a back. Some chairs have armrests. A chest of drawers goes all the way to the floor, while the space below a table is open. Who is going to use the furniture? Is it for children or grown-ups? Is it going into a formal room or a playroom? Is it fun and funky or understated?

 ## USABILITY
DOES THE FURNITURE ALLOW US TO DO WHAT WE NEED TO DO?
The "right" furniture depends on whom it's for. Is a love seat in your living room enough for you and a parent? Do you need a single bed or are bunk beds and futons right for your family? Is the furniture strong enough to stand up to family games or is the only activity quiet reading?

 ## ERGONOMICS
DO ALL THE PARTS WORK TO MAKE FURNITURE SAFE AND COMFORTABLE?
Industrial designers make ergonomics a priority when it comes to furniture. A car seat is shaped like a shell with padded upholstery to keep a child safe and comfortable. A sofa has a sturdy wood frame that shapes it and makes it strong enough for more than one person to sit on at the same time.

☑ AESTHETICS

DOES IT LOOK GREAT?

Taste for styles of furniture can range from fussy to simple. It has to look good if people are going to buy it. Industrial designers have to predict changes – or set trends – in taste.

☑ IS IT GREEN?

Designers aim to make each type of furniture attractive, unique, and ergonomic. The most popular material for furniture is wood. Recently, designers have learned how to use other materials, such as plastic, for furniture. Plastic can be molded into different shapes and dyed in many colors. Because it doesn't absorb water, it's great for outdoor furniture. Designers are analyzing what will leave a lighter footprint – wood or plastic.

NEAT MATTRESSES – NO MORE BUGS!

Cast-iron beds and cotton mattresses were not invented until the 18th century. The mattresses used today are made of steel coil springs and rubber or synthetic foam. When you lie down, your body presses down on the coils, and the coils push back. This action supports your spine's natural curves so your back feels good and you wake up feeling rested.

THUMBS UP! *THE EAMES CHAIR*

The Eames lounge chair is one of the most famous chairs ever produced. It was designed in the 1950s by designers Charles and Ray Eames. They worked on this chair for many years to make it as comfortable, sturdy, and beautiful as possible. The Eames Chair is made of three curved plywood shells. The leather seat cushions are the same shape as the shells, so they fit together perfectly. The backrest and headrest are screwed together, and the whole unit is suspended on the seat so that the chair can move back and forth. All the screws, clips, and rings that hold the chair together are hidden, so the wood and leather stay smooth. The footrest can be used separately or pulled up to the chair.

WHAT'S THE GLITCH?
ERGONOMICS

Most folding chairs are uncomfortable because they don't have adequate back support. The seats are not contoured, and the backrests are too narrow. Because the legs are very thin, the chair is not stable, and you may find yourself wobbling back and forth or even tipping over.

THINK LIKE AN INDUSTRIAL DESIGNER

You may not be able to design your own chair, but you can control the way you sit. Ergonomic seating promotes a comfortable working posture that prevents your back and neck from hurting and eases eyestrain. To sit ergonomically, your body should be aligned from your head to your toes. Sit with your hands, wrists, and forearms in a straight row. Your head should be in line with your upper body and should be slightly bent toward the computer. Your eyes should be level with the screen. Relax your shoulders and keep your upper arms at your sides, with your elbows bent close to your body. Now you are sitting and working ergonomically.

CHAPTER SIX

BRIGHT IDEAS: DESIGN FOR LIGHTING

THE WAY IT WAS....

Before we had artificial lighting, people had to complete their daily tasks in daylight. After sundown, they were often at risk, becoming the hunted, rather than the hunter. The first method of artificial lighting is thought to have been bundles of sticks tied together to make torches to light up caves or to help people see at night while moving from place to place.

Approximately 15,000 years ago, people learned how to make oil lamps. These lamps were made of natural materials such as hollow rocks, stones, animal horns, and, later, pottery. The lamps were filled with oil made from vegetables or animal fat and lit by a fiber wick. Olive oil was also commonly used because it was widely available and cheap. Oil lamps are still used today, but now we mainly use paraffin or kerosene.

In the late 1700s, people discovered that gas from petroleum and coal would burn. Gas lamps soon became popular for use in homes and outdoors. In 1879, Thomas Edison invented the incandescent electric lightbulb. Although electricity was already being used, no one had figured out how to use it as a source of lighting. After two years of trying, Edison covered a piece of sewing thread with carbon, put it in a glass bulb, and connected it to an electric source. The thread glowed for forty hours!

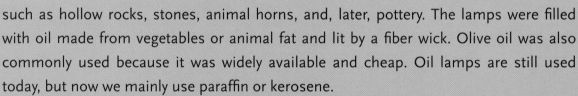

THE WAY IT IS NOW....

LAMPS, LIGHTING FIXTURES, AND MORE LAMPS

Edison's invention changed the world. Lighting became available at any time in homes, offices, schools, and other buildings.

An energy-efficient lighting system provides the best brightness but reduces the amount of energy used. To determine what kind of bulb it will need, designers must know how the light fixture will be used. Next, they think about the aesthetics. What will the fixture look like? What materials will work best for the purpose of the lamp? Metals are good because they reflect light. Aluminum is lighter than steel and can be spun into many different shapes. Heat in light fixtures is measured in wattages. Every lamp comes with instructions that include the maximum watt bulb that can be used in the fixture, without damaging it or starting a fire.

OUTDOOR LIGHTING

Outdoor lighting is important because it creates a safe environment for drivers and pedestrians. Early streetlights were lit by gas. The first gas lamps appeared in London, England, in 1807. Every night at dusk, a lamplighter would tour the town and light all the lamps. The first electric streetlights were developed by Pavel Yablochkov, in 1876.

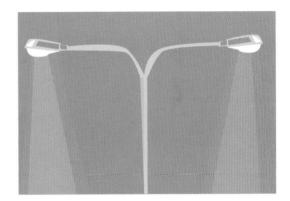

Many types of outdoor lighting are used to illuminate streets and roadways, to decorate outdoor settings, and to light up buildings. The fixture's style should fit into its surroundings and meet the standards of local building codes for safety and energy consumption.

- **Roadway lights illuminate signs that are outside the range of a car's headlights.**

- **Streetlights provide high-intensity lighting for busy streets.**

- **Security lighting is used to brighten up the entrances of homes or public buildings.**

A *Lighting Design* Checklist

☑ **FORM AND FUNCTION**

DOES IT REFLECT WHAT YOU USE IT FOR?

What should a light fixture look like? Even if it's fun and funky, like a bear-shaped fixture for a child's room, it should still provide adequate lighting.

☑ **USABILITY**

DOES IT DO WHAT YOU NEED IT TO?

Designers are concerned with how light is distributed around a room through a fixture. Most of a bulb's brightness is captured inside the fixture, so designers want to make sure as much light as possible can be streamed out.

TURN OFF YOUR NIGHT-LIGHT

Your room should be as dark as possible when you go to sleep. Light suppresses our natural melatonin, a chemical that our body releases to tell us that we are tired. Darkness triggers the melatonin, so we can relax and fall asleep.

HOW DOES AN INCANDESCENT LIGHTBULB WORK?

When electricity flows through a strand inside of a lightbulb, the strand resists the electricity. The resistance makes the strand heat up, making it glow and give off light. Only ten percent of the energy in an incandescent bulb produces light. The other ninety percent is heat.

☑ ERGONOMICS

DO ALL THE PARTS WORK TO MAKE IT SAFE AND EFFICIENT?

Lights should have controls that are identifiable and easy to use, and they should be safe. Exposed bulbs are dangerous, especially around small children.

☑ AESTHETICS

DOES IT LOOK GREAT?

Lighting should reflect the decor of the room it's in. Is it traditional or modern, casual or formal? A crystal chandelier looks great in a ballroom, but it would look silly in your bedroom.

☑ IS IT GREEN?

Designers create lights that use controls such as dimmers and automatic timers; that way, the light can be adjusted. Lighting technology has changed dramatically, as more energy-efficient products are developed. Halogen bulbs cost slightly more than incandescent bulbs, but they use fifteen percent less energy and last two to four times longer. Fluorescent tubes use sixty percent to eighty percent less energy and last ten to twenty times as long as incandescent lightbulbs, but they don't work in standard light sockets. Compact fluorescent lights (CFLs) do fit into standard light sockets, and they use almost seventy-five percent less energy and can last up to ten times longer than incandescent bulbs.

THUMBS UP!
TUNGSTEN-HALOGEN LIGHTBULBS

Tungsten-Halogen bulbs are similar to regular bulbs, but they use a lot less energy and last two to four times longer. They give off a whiter light than traditional bulbs and come in a variety of shapes and sizes that can be used in most indoor and outdoor lighting fixtures. They do, however, get very hot, so only use them in fixtures made of porcelain or plastic materials that can withstand high temperatures.

WHAT'S THE GLITCH?
IT USES TOO MUCH ENERGY

When the incandescent lightbulb was invented, it was an amazing product that changed the way people live. Today, however, it is a poor choice because it uses too much power. Incandescent bulbs waste ninety percent of the energy they consume. If you want to think "green," you should choose another kind of bulb.

THINK LIKE AN INDUSTRIAL DESIGNER

AUDIT YOUR HOME LIGHTING

Saving energy is a good way to start "going green." With your parents, check all the lightbulbs in your house. Do you have 100-watt bulbs in fixtures where 60- or 75-watt bulbs would give enough light? If you have places where the lights are on for long periods of time, you can replace standard bulbs with more energy-efficient compact fluorescent lights. These changes will save money on your electric bill and conserve energy.

COLOR RENDERING INDEX (CRI)
Levels of brightness are measured by the Color Rendering Index (CRI). The highest CRI is 100, which is as close to natural daylight as it is possible to reach. The lower the CRI, the harder it is to tell colors, such as brown and blue or yellow and green, apart.

CHAPTER SEVEN

STORIES TO TELL, STORIES TO HEAR, AND STORIES TO KEEP: DESIGN FOR COMMUNICATIONS

THINK OF THE MANY WAYS WE COMMUNICATE. An army of industrial designers, engineers, and inventors stand behind each telephone, television, computer, and camera.

THE WAY IT WAS....

People used to only communicate with drawings, by writing, and by talking in person. Then amazing inventions changed everything; from the way we read, write, talk, and record visual images.

In 1436, Johannes Gutenberg invented the printing press with moveable letters. The Gutenberg Press meant that books and newspapers could be reproduced inexpensively, and ordinary people could buy them and learn about the world. In 1874, the Sholes & Glidden Type Writer was invented, and it was the first one with a QWERTY keyboard (named for where the letters are placed), which is still used today. Its inventor, Charles Sholes, manufactured the typewriter through the Remington Company, making it the standard typewriter of its time.

For thousands of years, the only way to record an image was to draw it. Rock paintings found in caves have been dated back approximately 40,000 years. No one knows who painted them, but they show that ancient people used visual images to communicate. Then in the late 1800s and early 1900s, a series of inventions changed the world.

The Way It Is Now....
FROM TYPEWRITERS TO COMPUTERS

Today, most writing or "word processing" is done on computers. The first processors were adding machines. Scientists and engineers were the only people to use them, until 1936, when Konrad Zuse invented the first computer. At first, computers were so large that they took up a whole room. In 1972, the Hewlett Packard Company introduced a desktop All-In-One for scientists and engineers, not for use at home. In 1975, Bill Gates introduced the IBM desktop computer. It was smaller than the All-In-One, and came with a built-in, 5-inch monitor and a tape to store files. But at $10,000, ordinary people couldn't afford one.

In 1976, Steve Jobs and Steven Wozniak created an inexpensive desktop computer, naming it, and their company, after the legendary apple from the tree of knowledge. A year later, they introduced an easy-to-use compact version that came with a "mouse" that moved a curser on the screen and a floppy disc to store information. In 1981, IBM came out with a desktop computer, called the IBM Personal Computer or PC. Soon people were calling all desktop computers that weren't made by the Apple Corporation, PCs.

The Internet, and the way we use it, is constantly changing. Now we can remotely access the Internet on cellphones and laptops, small lightweight computers that are designed to be portable and open like a book. We can even get wireless access, allowing us to access the Internet without a cable connection. We can go online almost anywhere: "hot spots" can be found in hotels, cafes, airports, and other public spaces.

SMILE AND SAY "CHEESE"
CAMERAS

In 1835, Louis Jacques Daguerre invented a process that allowed him to create a fixed image that did not fade. This type of photograph is called a *Daguerreotype*.

The first cameras were large contraptions that were usually made of wood. They had a lens that let in light and a slot at the back to insert glass plates to capture the image. Cameras were too big, bulky, and expensive for average people, so they were used mostly by professional photographers.

Then George Eastman designed the Kodak camera, which revolutionized photography. It sold for $25, which was considered expensive at the time.

WHAT CAME NEXT?

The technology has changed much since the days of Eastman's Kodak camera. Today, you can hold a camera in the palm of your hand. Modern cameras are now ergonomically designed to be *user-friendly*. And they now come in both film and digital models. Digital cameras are miniature computers.

WHO DESIGNS WHAT PARTS?

All electronic equipment such as computers, cell phones, and televisions have both hardware and software. Industrial designers design the hardware, which is the part you see. Electronic engineers develop the software that's inside – components such as microchips that make the equipment work.

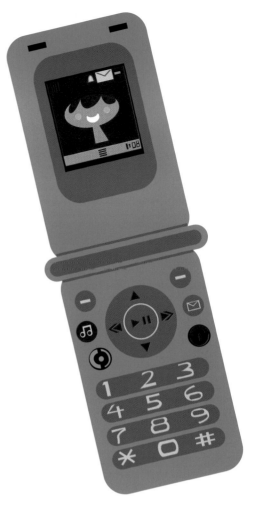

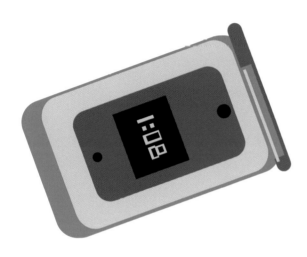

YAKETY-YAK, PLEASE TALK BACK!
TELEPHONES

Telephones weren't invented until the late 1800s, and it wasn't common for people to have them in their homes until the 1920s. Alexander Graham Bell introduced the first commercial telephone in 1877. It looked like a small box camera. And in 1879, he founded the Bell Telephone Company in New York City to produce and sell his phones. An early telephone was a wooden box with a metal mouthpiece and an earpiece attached to it by a wire. It had no dials or buttons. The caller picked up the receiver and spoke to an operator, who placed the call.

In 1878, Almon Brown Strowger introduced automatic direct dialing, which allowed phone subscribers to call each other directly. This technology eventually led to the introduction of Touch-Tone dialing in 1963. Touch-Tone phones had a base that had buttons with numbers from 0-9 for dialing.

A Communications Design Checklist

☑ ## FORM AND FUNCTION
DOES IT REFLECT WHAT YOU USE IT FOR?

Can you tell if the product is a camera, a cell phone, a computer, or all three? What are the features that define it and communicate its purpose? How is a camera used to take photos different from one that shoots videos? And what about cameras that do both? What size is the lens? What does that tell you about the kind of photos it takes? The hardware must reflect the purpose of the product.

☑ ## USABILITY
DOES IT GIVE US GREAT RESULTS?

How easy or difficult is it to use? Is it small enough and easy to carry? Is it sturdy or are there sharp edges or small pieces that can break off? Is the product well insulated so it doesn't overheat when in use? Is it lightweight so you can take it with you wherever you go?

☑ ## ERGONOMICS
IS IT COMFORTABLE AND EASY TO USE?

To make an instrument easy to use, the designer figures out which buttons, such as *on* and *off*, are most important. Those buttons are always up front. Less important buttons, such as *reset* are placed away from the center, so you don't accidentally hit them.

AESTHETICS
DOES IT LOOK GREAT?

What does the product look like? Is it a fun color? Do you need a carrying case or can you slip it into your pocket? Is it sleek and smooth?

IS IT GREEN?

Is the product energy efficient? Does it use a rechargeable battery? If it uses batteries, how many does it use, and how often do you have to change them? Does it have a lot of unnecessary parts or is it sleek with a minimum of materials? If it's an instant camera, is the plastic recyclable?

COMPUTER AIDED DESIGN

You see the results of Computer Aided Design (CAD) every time you watch an animated film or play a video game. CAD software has changed the way industrial designers work. Now, using a mouse and keyboard commands, designers can see their designs from any angle by zooming in or out, rotating the image, or standing it on its head. CAD allows the designer to make changes on a three-dimensional computer image before giving the drawings to the model maker.

THUMBS UP!

The most popular telephone ever designed was by Henry Dreyfuss. He designed the Model 500 for Bell Telephone Laboratories in 1949. It was plastic instead of wood or metal. Dreyfuss improved on earlier designs by placing the numbers outside the finger holes and molding them into the plastic, instead of printing them on the surface of the dial. That way, they wouldn't wear off. Molding them into the plastic also made them *tactile*, meaning you could feel them. This feature cut down on the number of wrong numbers dialed. Dreyfuss designed the phone with sleek, clean lines. At first, it was only available in black, but soon, Bell began making it in colors like cream and red. In the 1960s, when Touch-Tone or push-button dialing was developed, Dreyfuss replaced the dial with plastic buttons.

WHAT'S THE GLITCH?
ERGONOMICS

Most cell phones are examples of bad ergonomic design. In order to use them, you have to raise your arm to your ear, which is an unnatural position. Using an earpiece will allow you to talk without holding the phone and helps alleviate the problem of arm fatigue.

THINK LIKE AN INDUSTRIAL DESIGNER

Before a designer starts a project, he or she studies other products already on the market. Look at different kinds of cell phones. What features do you like? What don't you like?

Now draw the outline of a cell phone on a piece of cardboard or Bristol board. What does it look like? How big is it? What size are the buttons? Is it a flip-top or a one-piece? Are you using symbols such as arrows, or words for the *on* and *off* buttons? What color is the phone?

Remember, designers draw many versions of a product before they choose a final design, so you should do the same. When you have a sketch that you prefer, cut it out and hold it in your hand. Is it the right size? Do your fingers fit on the buttons? Can you read the numbers and letters? Is the screen big enough for you to see?

Make a model of your phone from clay or play dough. Use your cutout for the pattern and then use the cutout as the phone's face. Now you have a model cell phone that you can show to your "boss."

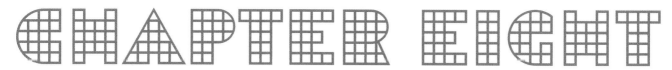
SHOW TIME: DESIGN FOR ENTERTAINMENT

THE WAY IT WAS....

Guglielmo Marconi was an Italian inventor who developed a radiotelegraph system and set up the world's first radio station on the Isle of Wight in England in 1899. Radio

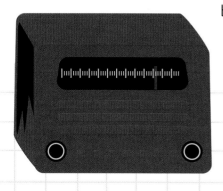

became popular in the 1900s, and by the end of the 1930s, radios were common in homes. People listened to their favorite programs such as "Superman," "The Lone Ranger," and "The Shadow," with the same attention that we give to television today. During World War II, radio was a major source of news.

Early radios were large because the cabinets held bulky equipment. In 1960, the Japanese company Sony invented the transistor radio that was small enough to be carried in a purse or pocket.

THE WAY IT IS NOW....

Today, radios come in many shapes, sizes, and styles. They continue to be popular for music, news, and sports broadcasts, but most people enjoy their favorite dramas and comedy shows on television.

TELEVISION

The birth of television occurred around 1928, when the U.S. Federal Radio Commission issued the first television station license. However, in 1936 there were only about 200 television sets in use in the entire world!

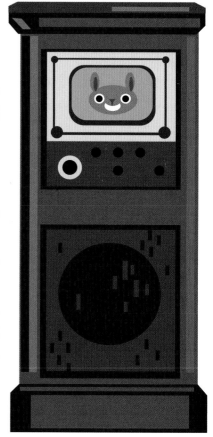

During the 1930s radio stations such as CBS (Columbia Broadcast System) in the United States and the BBC (British Broadcasting Corporation) in London began to develop television transmission. The work was largely stopped during the Second World War. But after the war, television development boomed.

Early televisions had small screens, but the mechanical parts were bulky so the sets were housed in large cabinets. Pictures were black-and-white and often blurry. There were only a few stations until the 1950s. Programming increased and new features such as large screens, color pictures, and remote controls were introduced. As the technology improved, the television cabinets became smaller and sleeker.

Today there are hundreds of stations and programs. You can tune in on a large digital screen, your computer, or even on your cell phone.

MOTION PICTURES

After cameras were invented, scientists noticed that when you flip through a sequence of still photos, the images you see appear to move. They wondered if it was possible to develop a camera that would take "moving pictures."

Soon other inventors were experimenting with camera technology. In France, Auguste and Louis Lumiére developed the Cinematographe, a lightweight, handheld camera that included a processing unit to develop the film and a projector to view the moving pictures. Then in 1895 and 1896, the brothers made the first of many short films depicting true-life situations.

Around the same time, inventors Charles Jenkins and Thomas Armat designed a projector called the Vitascope. Together with Thomas Edison, the brothers manufactured their product, and the Vitascope became the first commercial projector in the U.S. By 1901, Edwin Porter, who worked for Edison, began making longer films that actually told a story. *The Great Train Robbery* was the first full-length feature film to be screened.

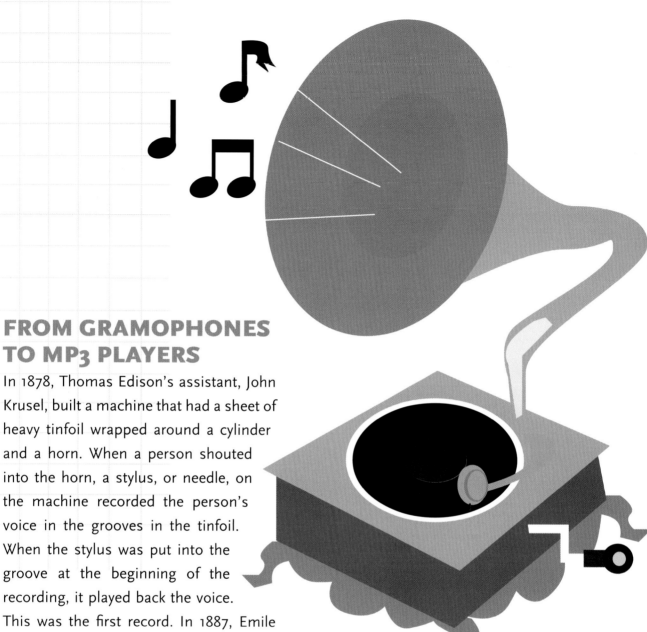

FROM GRAMOPHONES TO MP3 PLAYERS

In 1878, Thomas Edison's assistant, John Krusel, built a machine that had a sheet of heavy tinfoil wrapped around a cylinder and a horn. When a person shouted into the horn, a stylus, or needle, on the machine recorded the person's voice in the grooves in the tinfoil. When the stylus was put into the groove at the beginning of the recording, it played back the voice.

This was the first record. In 1887, Emile Berliner introduced the Gramophone. His machine used wax discs with circular grooves to record the sound, and it had an arm with a stylus, a horn to transmit the sound, and a turntable for the record to sit on.

As technology improved, designers replaced the horn with speakers built into the box, making phonographs, or record players, smaller and easier to use. Records had a large hole in the center to drop onto the player. Later disks were made of vinyl and that's when record players really took off. Wax melts at low temperatures so it wasn't very practical. Vinyl melts at really high temperatures, and once it cools and hardens, it stays that way.

Magnetic tape was invented in the 1930s to record sound. The original tape came on large reels, similar to those used for film. These tapes were called reel-to-reel because the tape is fed from one reel, onto a second reel. In the 1960s, Philips invented compact reel-to-reel tapes that fit into a plastic cassette. But it was the invention of the pre-recorded tape cassette that enabled Sony to develop the Walkman, a portable tape player that people can listen to while they walk, run, or jog. Later models played a compact disc (CD) instead of a tape.

One product often leads to another, and technology has changed so much that we now listen to electronic music files instead of records or tapes or even CDs. Personal media players (PMPs) are portable electronic devices that store and play back digital media (music, television shows, movies, books, etc.).What technology do you think will come next?

An *Entertainment Design* **Checklist**

☑ **FORM AND FUNCTION**

DOES IT LOOK LIKE IT DOES WHAT IT'S MEANT TO?

Today it's easy to be confused about the functions of communication equipment. But you can still tell the difference between a cell phone, television, or computer by its form. Television sets are big; cell phones fit into the palm of your hand. Form still dictates the primary purpose of a product.

☑ **USABILITY**

CAN YOU USE IT FOR THE PURPOSE IT WAS INTENDED?

How big is your TV screen? Are the buttons on the remote control clearly marked? What about the buttons on your cell phone? Is it easy to use them? Is the screen big enough to see the number you are dialing? How does the equipment work?

☑ **ERGONOMICS**

DO ALL THE PARTS WORK SAFELY AND EFFICIENTLY?

Are all the parts safe and easy to use? Are the cords to equipment such as stereos and televisions hidden so you don't trip over them? Are the products well insulated so they don't overheat when you use them?

AESTHETICS
DOES IT LOOK GREAT?

Does the design of your television fit into your family room or living room? If it's part of a system that includes other components such as speakers, do they look like they were designed to fit together?

IS IT GREEN?

Are your televisions and other electronic devices energy-saving models? When you're ready to replace them, are they recyclable?

THOMAS EDISON (FEBRUARY 11, 1847 – OCTOBER 18, 1931)
Thomas Edison was kicked out of school at the age of seven because he asked too many questions. His mother educated him at home, and by age twelve, Edison had a job selling newspapers on trains.

His first invention was an electric vote-recording machine. He couldn't sell it, but he did sell his next invention — an improved version of the stock-ticker machine used in the stock market. In 1876, he opened a laboratory in Menlo Park, New Jersey, where he invented the first phonograph and the incandescent lightbulb. In 1887, he moved to a larger laboratory in West Orange, where he became involved in early motion picture development. His other inventions include a storage battery, the Dictaphone, and a mimeograph machine. In 1892, he started the General Electric Company. During his lifetime, Edison held over 1,000 patents. His original laboratory is now in the Greenfield Village Museum in Michigan, and his home and laboratory in West Orange is a national historic site.

and could store more media files than other brands. It is sleek, attractive, and user-friendly. It has five simple control buttons on a navigation wheel, which allows users to scroll easily through electronic files. Apple has introduced new-and-improved iPod models with increased functions and even greater design features, but its five-buttoned control concept has yet to change.

THUMBS UP!
APPLE IPOD

The first personal media player was invented by a South Korean company in 1998. Many would follow, but none would be as successful as the Apple iPod, introduced in 2001. With other PMPs, users had to transfer their music files directly from CDs to their computers, then transfer the files to their music players. People began file-sharing over the Internet, which led to illegal downloading. Apple revolutionized the media-player business by introducing the iTunes software. The software allowed users to buy music (and other media files) for download directly from the Apple online store to their computers. Through iTunes, Apple can monitor the media files, protecting the company and the copyright owner of the files from piracy. It wasn't long before Apple also introduced a version of iTunes for PCs, making them the number one choice for PMPs. The iPod was more compact than most other media players

WHAT'S THE GLITCH?
ERGONOMICS

Poor product design often happens when companies copy or "knock off" a successful product. Because they want to sell it cheaper than the original, they use inferior materials and do not spend the time or money to design the details, such as buttons and headsets that make the original product unique. After Sony's success, many Walkman knockoffs appeared on the market. Most of these portable cassette players lacked the Walkman's design sophistication.

THINK LIKE AN INDUSTRIAL DESIGNER

MAKE A FLIP-BOOK MOVIE

In the past, animators used flip books to make their action figures move. You can see how they did it by making your own moving pictures. You'll need a stack of 3" x 5" blank index cards, a rubber band, and a black Magic Marker. If you want to use color, dark shades show up best. On a separate sheet of paper, draw the whole picture you want to show in your movie. Study your image to see how you can break it down into stages of motion. Then draw each stage on the end of the index cards. The movement changes should be gradual, so that when you flip the cards, the action will appear natural. When you have completed each step, stack the cards and secure them in the middle with the rubber band. Your pictures should be on the same end of each card. Now flip the cards and watch your movie!

PIXAR

Pixar was started by Steve Jobs, who also founded the Apple Computer Company. From the start, design has been a major component in all its productions. In 1979, Jobs bought the computer graphics division of George Lucas' Lucasfilm. He named the division Pixar and started making short films. The company went on to create the award-winning Computer-Assisted Production System (CAPS). With that technology, in 1995, Pixar released *Toy Story*, the first completely computer-animated film, which won an Academy Award.

CHAPTER NINE

FUN STUFF: DESIGN FOR TOYS

THE WAY IT WAS....

Long ago, children played with toys and games that helped them to learn life skills or prepare for their future careers. Back then, most kids would grow up to work in the same profession as their parents, so most of their toys were smaller versions of tools that their parents used at work. Many toys that children played with in the past helped them to think on their feet, make decisions, and trust their instincts.

Until modern times, most toys were homemade. Children in Ancient Greece and Rome played with balls, clay rattles, dolls, hoops, and spinning tops, and they played outdoor games such as tag and hide-and-seek. Children often made their own toys from common objects such as pebbles, barrel hoops, and scraps of cloth. In later years, wealthy families were able to buy their children intricately handcrafted toys such as building blocks, hobby horses, and dolls with porcelain faces and fancy clothes.

THE WAY IT IS NOW....

By the 1900s, companies began mass-producing toys, making them cheaper to buy than the handmade ones. Some of the most popular were toy soldiers, farmyard and zoo animals, and model trains. Most children had one or two favorite toys: girls usually had a special doll; boys usually had a set of soldiers or cowboys. By the mid-1900s, many companies were making a wide variety of toys and games. Children are still playing with some of those same toys today.

FRISBEE

The Frisbee was originally a tin pie plate. The Frisbie Baking Company of Bridgeport Connecticut baked pies for many local colleges. The students ate the pies, then took the plates to the park and tossed them back and forth. In 1948, Walter Morrison and Warren Franscioni invented a plastic version of the pie plate and changed the spelling to Frisbee. In 1957, a new toy company called Wham-O bought the toy and Frisbees have been flying through the air ever since.

SLINKY

The Slinky was designed in 1945 by Richard James; a Navy engineer who noticed that when a metal spring fell down onto the ship's deck, it flip-flopped. He thought it would be fun to make a toy that did the same, so after the war, he and his wife, Betty, figured out how to coil a long, steel ribbon into a spiral. They named their new toy Slinky. The Slinky became so popular that it is still sold today. The only change to the original design was to make it safer by creasing the ends of the wire, so they aren't pointy and sharp.

ROLLER SKATES — A STORY ON WHEELS

The story of roller skates is a good example of how a design changes over the years. In 1819, Monsieur Petibledin was the first person to receive a patent for an in-line skate, which had four rollers nailed in a straight line to a wooden sole that fit on the bottom of a shoe. Then in 1863, an American, James Plimpton, made a pair of skates called the *quad* skate. Each skate had four wheels — two under the ball of the foot and two under the heel. The wheels had rubber springs, so a person could skate forwards, backwards, and turn. This was the start of modern skates.

In 1876, Englishmen William Brown and Joseph Henry Hughes designed adjustable ball-bearing wheels. Ball bearings reduce friction and make the wheels turn faster and smoother. Their design is the basis for modern skate and skateboard wheels. About the same time, another designer, E.H. Barney, invented a clamp-on system for attaching skates to a shoe or boot. The clamps were tightened with a key to keep the skates from falling off. Before that, skates were attached with leather straps that broke off easily. Another innovation was the toe stop. Even after the shoe skate or "skating boot" was introduced, people continued to use clamp-on skates until the late 1950s.

Brothers Scott and Brennan Olson revived in-line skating in the 1980s. They changed the design by using five polyurethane wheels, attaching the wheels to ice-hockey boots, and adding a rubber toe break. With their new-and-improved skates, the Olson brothers started their company, Rollerblade Inc.

A *Toy Design* Checklist

Toy designers often describe themselves as grown-up children who create toys they would like to play with. But toy designers have a lot to think about.

☑ FORM AND FUNCTION

DOES IT REFLECT WHAT IT'S MEANT TO DO?

Does a truck look like a truck? Does a train run on tracks? Do the pieces of a puzzle fit together?

☑ USABILITY

DOES IT DO WHAT YOU NEED IT TO DO?

Not all toys are right for children of all ages. Is it right for the age and ability of the child using it? Are there too many pieces or just enough? Is it easy to understand?

☑ ERGONOMICS

DO ALL THE PARTS WORK SAFELY?

What material is the toy made of? Materials must be free of lead and other poisonous substances. For example, fabrics used for dolls' clothes must be flame-retardant, and toys should not be made with small, loose parts that a child could swallow.

WHY ARE MOST TOYS PLASTICS?

Before the 1940s, toys were made of wood, metal, cloth, clay, and other common materials. Dolls' faces were often porcelain. Plastic changed the toy industry because it was a material that could be molded into all kinds of colorful shapes, and the molds enabled manufacturers to make many toys at a time, rather than only a few at a time. Lead-free colors are used in the plastic so there is no paint for a child to chip off and swallow. Plastic toys won't rust or splinter, and they have smooth, rounded edges that won't scratch.

MATTEL TOYS

In 1945, Ruth and Elliot Handler started Mattel Toys by making dollhouses from leftover wood scraps. The dollhouses were such a success they decided to make other toys. In 1947, the Handlers introduced a ukulele called the Uke-A-Doodle. After that, they introduced the Burp Gun, an automatic cap pistol. They soon started making three-dimensional dolls for little girls. They named the doll Barbie, after their daughter. Barbie was a huge success and the Handlers used the money to expand and develop many new toys. In 1961, the Ken doll became Barbie's boyfriend. Ken is named after the Handlers' son.

In 1968, Mattel introduced a line of miniature candy-colored metal hot rods that came on specially designed plastic tracks. Other brands of model cars had wheels that didn't move. Using piano wires, which are thin and durable, Mr. Handler added axles and working wheels to the cars. The small diameter of the wheels generated minimum friction, so the cars could go downhill on very smooth plastic tracks at 300 miles per hour! When he saw it speeding along, Mr. Handler said, "Wow, those are hot wheels!"

 ## AESTHETICS
DOES IT LOOK GREAT?

Does the toy have bright colors and fun shapes that are easy to understand and use? Is it appealing to the age group for which it's intended? A ten year old wouldn't want to play with a baby's toy. What makes you choose a toy?

 ## IS IT GREEN?

Is the toy over-packaged – is there too much paper and plastic wrap to throw out? Does the toy work manually or does it use batteries? If so, what kind and how many? Is it sturdy enough to be handed down from one child to the next?

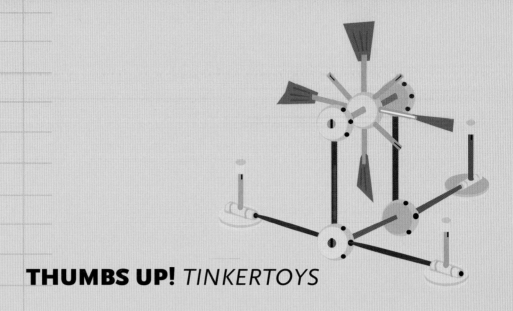

THUMBS UP! *TINKERTOYS*

Tinkertoy construction sets were invented in 1914 by Charles Pajeau, a stonemason from Illinois. As Pajeau watched children playing with pencils, sticks, and empty spools of thread, he began to imagine a construction kit for kids. So he got to work and made a set of long, round sticks and wooden wheels with holes in them that kids could connect together to make three-dimensional structures. But when he tried to sell his new toy, no one was interested. So, during the Christmas shopping rush, Pajeau hired midgets to wear elf costumes and play with his Tinkertoys in the window of a Chicago store. His creativity paid off.

People stopped to watch the "elves" play with the set, and then they bought the toy. Within one year, he had sold one million sets, and children are still playing with Tinkertoys today!

WHAT'S THE GLITCH?
IT'S DANGEROUS!

Any toy that has small magnets or other small parts that can break off is a badly designed toy. Magnets and small parts are a serious hazard for young children because they can choke on them. The U.S. Consumer Safety Product Commission lists magnets as one of the top five home hazards. The Commission recalls millions of toys every year because they include small magnets and other dangerous parts.

THINK LIKE AN INDUSTRIAL DESIGNER

You don't have to buy all your toys. There are many that you can make yourself.

BE A MODEL MAKER

Before a product is produced, the designer makes a three-dimensional model. Often, these models are sculpted from clay. You can make your own play dough and use it to sculpt models.

PLAY DOUGH RECIPE

250 ml (1 cup) flour
125 ml (1/2 cup) salt
10 ml (2 tsp.) cream of tartar
250 ml (1 cup) food coloring
15 ml (1 tbsp) vegetable oil

Mix all the ingredients together in a saucepan. With an adult's help, cook over medium heat for three minutes until it forms a ball. Carefully remove the dough from the pan and place it on a counter or table top. Let it sit for a few minutes until it is cool enough to handle. Knead the dough for two minutes, until it becomes smooth. Store it in a plastic bag.

Make several batches in different colors. Now you can use your play dough to model any invention you want.

CHAPTER TEN

A DESIGNER'S TOOLBOX

COMPUTER-AIDED DESIGN (CAD) PROGRAMS allow designers to create, change, and manipulate designs on the computer, before they become prototype models.

DRAWINGS show the product in detail.

PENS, PENCILS, AND PAPER are the tools designers use to draw their ideas. Even though designers work with computers, many still sketch their ideas first on paper.

MATERIALS are the substances that designers use, such as metal, plastic, and wood, in their products.

PLASTIC is a type of substance made from oil and mixed with other chemicals, which can be melted down and molded into products of almost any shape and size.

PROTOTYPE MODELS are scaled-down or full-sized representations of proposed products.

REFERENCE MATERIALS such as books, magazines, and the Internet are used by designers to research products.

RENDERINGS are lifelike, almost photographic, product illustrations.

SKETCHES are rough concept drawings of how products look. Before products are finished, designers put their ideas down on paper to visualize what their products will look like.

STORES aren't just places to shop. Designers visit them regularly to see what is already on the market and to decide how they can make their products different and/or better.

TEMPLATES (drawing aids) are forms that help designers draw shapes, such as curves and circles, and depict people in the right size or scale.

ACKNOWLEDGMENTS

Thanks to my husband, Paul, for introducing me to the world of design and sharing his knowledge with me while I wrote *Design It!* Thanks also to designers Helen Kerr of Kerr and Company, Scott Grant of Designforce, and Steve Copeland of Spark Innovations for sharing their time, insights, and product photos and information. And special thanks to my publisher, Kathy Lowinger, and my editor, Lauren Bailey, for helping me turn my love of design into this beautiful book.